A LIFETIME
OF RULES
ON DATING
WOMEN

Cover design: Mary Mazer, Art That Works, San Diego

Cover concept: Mike and Bree Drabicki

ISBN: 0-9646452-2-X

Additional copies available by calling 1-800-409-7277.

All other inquiries: 615-783-1668.

INTRODUCTION

Over the past fifteen years, the rules in this book have come about through valuable lessons we have learned from our mistakes and successes while dating women. It was only after we started writing them down that we realized how our few simple guidelines had grown into hundreds of surefire rules. However, every time we thought our list was complete, another woman would come along and teach us something new.

We realize that women are all different, but these suggestions offer consistency in almost every situation. We don't claim to have advanced degrees in Psychology or Sociology. We are just a couple of bachelors who jotted down a few notes. This book won't turn you (or us) into any Casanova, but might add some humor and insight into your next date. All it is is advice – take it or leave it. Good luck and enjoy the book.

THE AUTHORS

1. Don't confuse love with lust.

    —

2. Always date a woman with a sense of humor; in other words, someone you can laugh with.

    —

3. Don't call a girl the day after you meet her.   Make her think that you have a life, even if you don't.

    —

4. If fighting is what keeps your relationship exciting, she's not the right one for you.

   —

5. You need to be completely independent before entering a relationship.

   —

6. Take a date to dinner instead of lunch; you won't be as rushed.

   —

7. Never use
coupons
on a date.

8. Find a woman who is a good listener.

    —

9. Never raise your hand to a woman.

    —

10. If she wants her old boyfriend back, let her have him.

    —

11. Don't soak yourself in cologne.

    —

12. The less you divulge, the higher you raise her curiosity.

    —

13. Never date a girl whose father calls her princess.

—

14. Never let a woman manipulate you.

—

15. One critical remark will always overshadow a million compliments.

—

16. Never forget your friends because of a woman. Women come and go; good friends will be there forever.

—

17. Remember, when picking up on the best-looking girl in a bar, she's practically immune to it.

—

18. If a woman's eyes meet with yours, don't be the first to look away.

—

19. Exercise with your girlfriend.

—

20. If she cheats with you, she'll cheat on you.

—

21. Don't be afraid to kiss a girl; just make sure that it is mutual.

—

22. Dating a woman who is smarter than you is fine, but dating a woman who *thinks* she is smarter than you is a nightmare.

—

23. Don't spend a fortune on a woman. If she is interested in you, money won't be relevant.

—

24. Try to find a woman with a musical talent.

—

25. Too many compliments can translate into desperation.

—

26. The one day that you don't shave will be the day you meet the girl of your dreams.

—

27. Be wary of women who immediately burden you with their problems.

—

28. Be careful dating a girl who eats more than you.

—

29. Take a close look at the first thing a woman cooks for you.   It will be her best effort.

—

30. Remember: they tell their sisters *everything*.

—

31. Be confident, not cocky.

—

32. If you really like her, take her to church.

    —

33. Always open doors for a woman.

    —

34. Dating bimbos will make you appreciate nice girls.

    —

35. There is no place for PDA (public displays of affection)!

    —

36. The quickest way to get over a girl is to go to her wedding.

—

37. Women are always attracted to a puppy.

—

38. Remember, when you get married, things will change.

—

39. A little jealousy is healthy, but avoid extremely jealous women.

—

40. Never give her a key to your place,
    unless she lives there.

    —

41. Respect a woman, but make sure she
    earns it.

    —

42. Loneliness is a state of mind; solitude
    is a state of being.

    —

43. Never let your girlfriend check your
    phone messages.

    —

44. Don't drive yourself crazy wondering what a woman is thinking.

—

45. If she loves you today, don't count on it for tomorrow.

—

46. Don't be afraid to cry, just make sure no one sees you.

—

47. Let the woman dominate the conversation on your first date.

—

48. Be honest.

49. Deny, deny, deny.

50. If you feel like you are losing control of your relationship, give yourself time away from her to regain your composure.

—

51. You can't lose with a plant; sometimes flowers are too much.

—

52. Don't play games.   It's a no-win situation.

—

53. As great as she may seem, she is still only human.

—

54. Smoking won't make you more attractive to women.

—

55. Don't be a pawn in someone else's relationship; pawns are expendable.

—

56. Never let a girl drive your only vehicle, unless she's going to the store to get beer.

—

57. Don't date a body without a brain.

—

58. Don't date a brain without a body.

—

59. Give in on little issues so you can get your way when big issues come along.

—

60. If your girl cheats with another guy, buy him a beer. He saved you a lot of time and money on a big mistake.

—

61. If you're really desperate for a date, borrow your friend's baby and go to the mall.

—

62. Don't date people you work with. (Don't dip your pen in the company ink.)

—

63. Lingerie is a great gift that you both can enjoy.

—

64. Never beg.   It makes her lose respect for you, but even worse, it makes you lose respect for yourself.

—

65. Never stop looking.   Women are too beautiful.

—

66. It makes it tough on a relationship when she doesn't like your best friend.

—

67. Always keep her guessing.

—

68. Don't put her on a pedestal.   It just makes it easier for her to kick you in the head.

—

69. If she looks good wearing glasses, she'll probably look great with them off.

—

70. Watch out for preacher's daughters; they are the wildest.

—

71. The sexier the woman, the less she has to disclose.

—

72. Men and women speak the same language, but somehow words get lost in the translation.

—

73. Most women aren't impressed by fighting.

—

74. Don't fear rejection.   It's better to try and fail than never to try at all.

—

75. Telling a woman not to do something will often drive her to do the exact opposite.

—

76. Don't be too spontaneous with your emotions.

—

77. Never ask a girl out because you need to.   Ask her out because you want to.

—

78. Be cautious of women who have
    been engaged but never married.

    —

79. Don't date a woman with children,
    unless you don't mind being second
    on her list.

    —

80. Love blinds you.   Make sure you have
    a friend to help lead you along when
    you get lost.

    —

81. Don't listen to country music if you are already seriously depressed over a woman.

—

82. Never take advantage of a girl who has had too much to drink.

—

83. If you give your heart away, expect it back soon.

—

84. Never let a woman dress you, but always let her undress you.

—

85. Don't feel pressured into saying "I love you" just because she says it to you.

—

86. Never let a woman force feed you.

—

87. If you start seeing issues of *Bride's Magazine* around her place, run.

—

88. People should work to make a marriage succeed, but if you have to kill yourself in a dating relationship, it's not worth it.

—

89. Never wear black socks with tennis shoes.

—

90. A woman wants a man with direction.

—

91. Never lay it on the line and then back down.

—

92. If a relationship isn't good from the get-go, get going.

—

93. Never take a girl on a second date if she tells you she loves you on the first date.

—

94. Keep a black book and never let a girlfriend persuade you to throw it away.

—

95. Every accusation made against you will be believed in its entirety.

—

96. Wisdom doesn't come with age; it comes with experience.

—

97. When entering a relationship, look before you leap.

—

98. Never date a girl who wants to change you.

—

99. Jealousy doesn't show how much you care, but how much you lack trust.

—

100. Never let a woman lead you by the hand.

—

101. Don't be afraid to let a woman pay.

—

102. If you don't smoke, don't date a girl who does.

—

103. If you are
     lonely, get
     a dog.

104. If she makes the effort to say she doesn't care, more than likely, she does.

—

105. Treat a lady like a lady.

—

106. Treat a witch like a witch.

—

107. When just meeting a group of girls, never try to entertain more than one.

—

108. Athletic women are a must.

—

109. Anyone who thinks they have met the perfect woman will soon realize that there is no such thing.

—

110. Getting a haircut before a first date can be extremely dangerous.

—

111. Stay calm and collected, even if she blows your mind.

—

112. Don't go looking for something in a
     relationship that you don't want to
     find.

     —

113. Love from one isn't enough for two.

     —

114. Don't be too anxious to jump into a
     sinking boat to rescue her from her
     problems.

     —

115. It's proper to walk her to the door after a date; besides, she may have better plans.

—

116. Let her know how much you like her, but only occasionally.

—

117. Never date a woman who owns more than one cat.

—

118. Feel free to be yourself.

—

119. Before you get married, keep in mind
     that the rest of your life is a very long
     time.

     —

120. Try to meet women who have the
     same interests as you.   You may love
     the beach, but she may be allergic to
     the sun.

     —

121. Be cautious when trusting girls named
     Angel, Faith, or Hope.

     —

122. If you want to know what she will look like in the future, look at her mother.

—

123. Never date a woman whose ex~ has a key to her house.

—

124. Make sure she leads an independent life.

—

125. So many of them and so few of us!

—

126. A woman can give a man everything
     he needs except one thing – variety.

     —

127. Sometimes the greatest line is a
     straightforward introduction. If she
     likes you, she'll let you know.

     —

128. Make sure you are well-rested before a
     big date.

     —

129. You will never date a woman who
     you will regret not marrying.

     —

130. Never chase a woman.

—

131. The difference between a woman and an elephant is that an elephant eventually forgets.

—

132. If you pay for too much at first, it may become expected.

—

133. Say it in diamonds, say it in mink, but never, ever say it in ink.

—

134. Never open up immediately.

—

135. The only safe way is abstinence.

—

136. A woman who wants to celebrate your anniversary every month is on a time schedule to get married.

—

137. Never date a girl who is physically stronger than you.

—

138. Don't drink too much on a date.

—

139. Stand your ground.   Be as stubborn
     as you need to be.

—

140. Female friends are a must.

—

141. A gift of one rose has the same or greater value as a dozen.

142. Never date a girl who will answer the phone while making love.

—

143. Make sure that reservations aren't the only thing she can make for dinner.

—

144. Don't ever spend your last dollar on a woman.

—

145. Don't be a sucker.

—

146. Try to keep a balance in your relationship. Let her know you care, but not more than she does.

—

147. Remember to flush the toilet and put the seat down.

—

148. In a relationship, there is no such thing as never or forever.

—

149. The body fades, but the face will stay forever.

—

150. Don't go through life afraid to lose a woman. Relationships are similar to an investment. One day you have a loss and the next day a capital gain.

—

151. Any woman who watches soap operas all day has a reduced sense of reality.

—

152. When looking at two blondes, remember: a blonde is a blonde is a blonde.

—

153. A quiet woman is better than one who never knows when to stop talking.

—

154. Never eat corn on the cob on a date.

—

155. Believe your friends when they tell you that your girlfriend is screwing you over. That's why they're your friends.

—

156. A tactful insult can often humble the snobbiest of women. (Not guaranteed.)

    —

157. Never eat garlic and drink beer on a date. For the rest of the date, you'll be reminded of your dinner.

    —

158. Learning to cook at least one good meal is a great way to impress a date.

    —

159. Always keep an ace in the hole.   You never know when the cards will be stacked against you.

—

160. Don't kiss if you can't tell.

—

161. There are always two sides to a woman.   .

—

162. Be cautious of women who can drink more than you.

—

163. If a girl sleeps with you on the first date, take her out one more time.

—

164. Always keep a baseball cap handy.

—

165. There is nothing you can do married that you can't do single – except get a divorce.

—

166. It's always a good sign when a woman buys you a drink.

—

167. Don't let a woman tell you what to do; let her suggest.

—

168. As attractive as one girl may be, there is always one better.

—

169. Never, ever, ever wear a weenie bikini to the beach.

—

170. Don't burn any bridges. It's always best to keep your options open.

—

171. Don't be afraid to request a cute waitress.

—

172. Date a woman who likes sports.

—

173. Don't let a woman speak for you.

—

174. If her sister doesn't like you, move on quickly.

—

175. Women marry men hoping they will change. Men marry women hoping they won't.

—

176. If you find it difficult to resist her, make sure you can...at least once.

—

177. Cellular phones and beepers don't impress women.

—

178. Be cautious of women in baggy clothes.   There is usually a good reason for wearing them.

    —

179. Never date a woman who is obsessed with cleanliness.

    —

180. You'll be the last to know a woman's true feelings.

    —

181. A sexual relationship is not as emotional to a man as it is to a woman.

—

182. A woman who would lie to others would lie to you.

—

183. Men fall in love with their eyes. Women fall in love with their ears.

—

184. Don't be a woman's meal ticket.

—

185. Search for a nice sunset.

—

186. Don't use dating services.

—

187. Don't cover your car with bumper stickers.

—

188. A woman who whines doesn't deserve to be listened to.

—

189. Don't beat around the bush. It's a
     waste of time.

     —

190. Warn her about your shortcomings so
     that she only has herself to blame.

     —

191. Make sure she loves to fish if you love
     to fish.

     —

192. Never date a girl who gives you
     pointers while shooting pool.

     —

193. If you are interested in a girl you think might be involved with someone, ask her if she has a boyfriend. If she says not really, she probably likes you.

—

194. Use the dating constant: When X tells you how many men she has slept with, multiply that variable by five to get the correct answer.

—

195. Don't take advice from friends who are terminally single and say that it is by choice.

—

196. If going out with a girl requires finding a date for her friend, forget it.

—

197. Be cautious of women who constantly wear expensive jewelry.

—

198. If you are having a hard time getting over a girl, try imagining her on the toilet.

—

199. Never be the first one to say "I love you."

—

200. Music is a powerful means of setting the mood.

—

201. Never date a girl who has dated your brother.

—

202. The nicer the guy, the more he gets mistreated by women.

—

203. Never date a woman who sleeps with her dog.

—

204. Don't worry about growing old; men only grow more distinguished.

—

205. Ideally, search for a woman who is ambitious and constantly seeking to better herself.

—

206. Never date a girl who refuses to wear underwear.

—

207. Don't let her pry into your past.

—

208. Every relationship has a saturation point.   Everything you do from day one contributes to reaching that point.

—

209. There is no such thing as starting fresh.   You both go back with all your baggage.

—

210. Always wear a condom, especially if she says you don't need one.

—

211. Many women will tell their personal feelings to a total stranger before they will tell you.

—

212. The more two people have in common, the better their relationship.

—

213. There is not one woman on earth who is unattainable.

—

214. If one of these rules upsets her, it's probably true.

—

215. In reference to marriage, why buy a horse when you can ride for free?

—

216. A woman's hands can tell you more than just her marital status.

—

217. Women will often impose standards on you that they can never meet themselves.

—

218. Make sure that she understands that guys need time to bond together.

—

219. Don't date high-maintenance women.

—

220. You shouldn't just date a girl to forget another one, even though it may ease the pain temporarily.

—

221. If she asks your opinion on her cooking, her weight, or the way she dresses, she doesn't always want the truth.   Sometimes it can get you in trouble.

—

222. If you want to get to know your date, don't take her to the movies.

—

223. A jeep is always in style.

—

224. A good smile can open many doors.

—

225. Never buy a girl a drink if she asks you to.

—

226. Learn about wines.

—

227. Don't just talk to talk. Have something pertinent to say.

—

228. Stay away from married women.   It's not right and it can get you into a world of trouble.

—

229. Never compromise your values.

—

230. On a first date, eat light.

—

231. Learn how to dance; it can never hurt.

—

232. Don't appear desperate, even though you may be.

—

233. To women, everything you do will have a motive, so it is best to have one.

—

234. The fewer guys you have with you, the less apprehension a girl will have in approaching you.

—

235. If you drink a 12-pack and ask yourself if you should, then you shouldn't.

—

236. If you think you have met your future wife, take a trip to the beach with some single friends.

—

237. Never complain. It accomplishes nothing.

—

238. Never ask a woman what she is thinking.

—

239. A woman on your arm is bait for other fish.

—

240. Good judgment comes from experience.   Experience comes from bad judgment.

—

241. It's harder to turn lovers into friends than to turn friends into lovers.

—

242. Never tell a woman if you have money.

—

243. Never tell a woman if you don't have money.

—

244. Keep your finances personal. That's why they're yours.

—

245. There is no such thing as a completely content woman.

—

246. All women are professionals.   We've never met an amateur.

—

247. If you get something cheap, it won't last.

—

248. Candles can be great for more than just a romantic dinner.

—

249. To a woman, a relationship is like a bridge game. She's always trying to better her hand.

250. Just because a relationship is comfortable doesn't mean that it is good.

—

251. Love is when you can only think of one person.   Lust is when you can't think.

—

252. Don't give a woman the opportunity to choose between you and someone else. Be the first to bail out. If she comes back to you, the ball will be in your court.

—

253. Live with a girl before you marry her,
but make sure you pay the rent so you
can kick her out at any time.

—

254. It's better to go home alone than to
pick up just any woman.

—

255. Keep a balance between your work
and a relationship.

—

256. Whenever she is feeling generous
with money, it is usually yours.

—

257. If your relationship is no longer fun, what's the point?

—

258. Be wary of women who have a wallet full of credit cards.

—

259. Don't let the comfort of a relationship make you lazy.

—

260. Always have a firm handshake, even with women.

—

261. Never go out hoping to run into your
     ex-girlfriend.

     —

262. Whenever possible, avoid talking
     about long-term plans.

     —

263. Don't let a woman pave the way for
     your future.

     —

264. Everything you tell a woman – even in
     the greatest confidence – will be told
     upon break-up.

     —

265. Having grease drip off your hair was a thing to do in the Fifties.

—

266. Appear to be busy.

—

267. Never change your direction or your attitude about life over a woman. You are the man she was attracted to initially.

—

268. If you must propose, don't do it in front of other people.   Give her the opportunity to say no.

—

269. If you always have to spend money to have a good time with a woman, ask yourself how good it really is.

—

270. Women do not want to hear about the other women you have dated.

—

271. When entering a relationship, always keep one foot on the ground.

—

272. Don't live in the past.   The future is all you've got.

—

273. If a girl would sleep with you on the first date, don't deceive yourself into believing that she wouldn't do it with others.

—

274. Chew with your mouth closed.

—

275. You can't help feeling jealous
     sometimes, just don't let it show.

     —

276. You can tell her a million times that
     you're not ready for marriage, but it
     will never seem to register.

     —

277. Never sit and wait for a woman; your
     time should be more precious to you.

     —

278. If your relationship is better than ever, brace yourself.

—

279. Don't say "I love you" expecting a response.

—

280. If you get engaged, make sure you love her, but make damn sure she loves you more.

—

281. Attempt to date women who have the same religious beliefs as you.

—

282. Some women will love you forever or until the money runs out.

—

283. Never put anything past a woman.

—

284. Make sure she doesn't mind getting her hair wet.

—

285. Good intentions are not always enough.

—

286. Find a woman whose work ethic is as good as yours, especially when it comes to housework.

—

287. Never take a girl on a second date if she ordered lobster on the first.

—

288. Never settle for second best.

—

289. Choose a woman who likes to smile rather than one who doesn't.

—

290. Buying a girl a rose in a bar is a waste of your money.

—

291. Never dance alone.

—

292. Don't talk about yourself too much unless asked...and even then, keep it short.

—

293. Don't think that you can never do better.

—

294. If you get a reputation for dating trashy women, that's the only type of woman you'll get.

—

295. Never date a girl who uses more four-letter words than you do.

—

296. Dating a hypochondriac can drive you crazy.

—

297. Don't be afraid to eat off your date's plate, especially if you're still hungry.

—

298. Never apologize more than once.

—

299. Don't date a woman who wears too much make-up.

—

300. The wiser women are, the less they trust men.

—

301. Make sure what you feel are your true feelings and not just your feelings for the moment.

—

302. Remember who's boss.

—

303. Never stalk or harass a woman – it's a waste of time.   You could be playing golf instead.

—

304. Everyone needs a good friend to talk them out of running back to a woman.

—

305. Homosexuality is a great thing.   It leaves more women for us to date.

—

306. If you tell her that you're sorry, try to make it sound believable.

—

307. A woman is like a cat. If you run up to her she'll want to fight, but if you ignore her, she'll want to play.

—

308. No matter how intimate your relationship is, don't use baby talk.

—

309. Women remember everything you wish they didn't.

—

310. Pay close attention to how long it takes her to talk about her last boyfriend. The longer it takes, the better the chance he broke up with her.

—

311. There are two types of women – the ones you want and the ones you need.

—

312. The first guy a woman ever slept with will always be held dear to her, so don't fight it.

—

313. Being too anxious is one of the quickest ways to scare a woman off.

—

314. Our definition of insanity is to date the same kind of person and expect different results.

—

315. Women are natural detectives.   Don't forget that no clue goes unnoticed.

—

316. Don't give a woman everything she wants.

—

317. When it comes to an engagement, avoid setting a date because it will come around sooner than you expect.

—

318. A woman's past is your future.

—

319. Don't let a woman with a better bank account than yours manipulate your better judgment.

—

320. Buy a pair of cowboy boots.

—

321. When a woman is on the rebound from another relationship, don't get too involved with her.

—

322. There is no age limit to playing the fool.

—

323. Get to know a girl well enough before you set your buddy up with one of her friends.   Bad times are contagious.

—

324. If she can live without you, let her.

—

325. Watch out for women who can't get along with other women.

—

326. If you are getting serious and you want to know if she's the right woman, take a three-day road trip with her.

—

327. Don't remain in a relationship just because you're worried about the other person.

—

328. If another guy starts talking to your date, do not show your jealousy by getting in the middle of their conversation. It only makes you look insecure.

—

329. Be wary of women whose whole college goal is to attain an "Mrs." degree.

—

330. Never discuss any sexual details of your past with a woman.

—

331. You can't take your emotions back once they have been given away.

—

332. Make sure that earrings are only worn in your date's ears.

—

333. Just because it glitters doesn't mean it's gold.

—

334. Never date a woman who must always consult a committee of friends.

—

335. A woman will pass any test to catch a man, but the greatest test is the test of time.

—

336. Don't let a woman use sex as a tool to get what she wants.

—

337. Find someone you can respect.

—

338. As a general rule, women regard men exactly like they regard their fathers.   If they don't like their fathers, they usually don't like men.

—

339. If your values are not the same, it wasn't meant to be.

—

340. Phone calls can be forgotten quickly. Letters will stick in her mind a lot longer.

—

341. Fools rush into relationships.

—

342. If her pets must like you in order for her to date you, move on.

—

343. Have some good stories handy. Sometimes a woman ends up dating a guy she never would have imagined dating simply because he makes her laugh.

—

344. Infatuation is like a whirlwind. You don't know what's happened until you wake up in a tree.

—

345. Never let her talk you out of a good thing.

—

346. If you get a tattoo, make sure it's not your girlfriend's name. Girlfriends are temporary; tattoos aren't.

—

347. Never date a woman who is dependent on drugs.

—

348. Always say "God bless you" when she sneezes.

—

349. Kiss with finesse, not aggress.

—

350. If you are running late, make sure you call.

—

351. A relationship
      is the only job
      where you
      can't use
      references.

352. You know you've got it bad for her when nothing else matters.

—

353. If she never reaches over to unlock the door on your side of the car, it's a bad sign.

—

354. Don't forget an anniversary, birthday, or Valentine's Day. In general, these are much more important to women than to men.

—

355. Don't wear colored contacts.

—

356. Don't drink cocktails through a straw.

—

357. Love is the imagination triumphantly conquering your intelligence.

—

358. If you ask a girl to dance and she declines rudely, simply ask, "Why are you being so picky? I'm not."

—

359. You can't make yourself care about
someone; just let it happen.

—

360. Always read the newspaper and keep
up with current events.

—

361. A Harley-Davidson is cool, but it is
much cooler to be alive.

—

362. Always keep a mint or breath
freshener handy.

—

363. Remember the pain you overcame and dealt with in a previous relationship to ease any heartache you may feel today.

—

364. Don't call a girl on a miserable rainy day.

—

365. Having long hair is one thing, but having a tail just isn't going to cut it.

—

366. Never break up over the phone.

—

367. Highly dramatic women are great for movies, not relationships.

—

368. Never use your professional title in an introduction. Your first name should do just fine.

—

369. Save a few dollars in your wallet after a first date. At the end of the night you may need to buy a couple of drinks to either celebrate or forget the evening.

—

370. If you really want to go out with one particular woman, be her friend first. Let her get to know you for who you are without any pressure.

—

371. Don't wait till you have a date; always keep those nose hairs trimmed.

—

372. Tip generously, especially when on a date.

—

373. IF SHE LOVES
OLD WESTERNS,
YOU'VE GOT
YOURSELF ONE
HELL OF A
WOMAN.

374. Don't let your words be betrayed by your actions.

—

375. Women don't tell you their rules until after you've broken them.

—

376. A man is not complete until he is married, and then, he is finished.

—

377. Never wear chains outside of your collar.

—

378. Women dream about the things men fear – like security and settling down.

—

379. If you look good with a unibrow, you'll definitely look better with it plucked.

—

380. Don't dip or chew tobacco on a date.

—

381. Expectations amount to nothing.

—

382. Praying together is one of the greatest forms of intimacy.

—

383. Don't commit yourself on a blind date. Make plans to meet her out somewhere.

—

384. Air brushed T-shirts and license plates were never fashionable.

—

385. Without trust, what do you have?

—

386. To half the women, money is everything.   To the other half, it's only important if you don't have any.

—

387. Redheads are either stunningly attractive or they're not.   There's no gray area.

—

388. It's all in your attitude.

—

389. If you are going to break up, do it before her birthday or Christmas.

—

390. If a woman has you doing things you swore you'd never do, you are in trouble.

—

391. A man is always innocent until a woman proves him guilty.

—

392. Don't be threatened by a woman who makes more money than you. Be thankful.

—

393. If a relationship doesn't work the first time, it won't work the second.

—

394. It's never too late to stay single.

—

395. Seductive words should attract, not offend.

—

396. You can take the woman out of the trash, but you can't take the trash out of the woman.

—

397. Don't tell a woman all of your secrets, no matter how close you are.

—

398. Going bald isn't so bad unless you wear a cheap toupee.

—

399. If she cheats on you once, she's a fool. If she cheats on you twice, you're a fool.

—

400. Chasing women can sometimes be more fun than actually catching them.

—

401. When going out for the night, often the less time you spend on your appearance, the more women you will meet.

—

402. What you find the most attractive about a woman may be the thing that drives you craziest in the end.

—

403. Never date someone because it is convenient.

—

404. Never feel like you have to return compliments.

—

405. Never trust a woman to pick out another woman for you.

—

406. When a man is taken, he will encounter more flirtation than when he is single.

—

407. Don't say you do if you don't.

—

408. You gotta love 'em before you can really hate 'em.

—

409. Don't find someone you can live with. Find someone you can't live without.

—

410. Never let your girlfriend read this book.

—

411. NEVER TAKE ADVICE FROM GUYS WHO HAVE ENOUGH TIME TO WRITE HANDBOOKS.

BIOGRAPHIES

Louis Vale was born and raised in New Orleans. He received a degree in finance from Louisiana Tech and now lives in Lafayette, Louisiana, where he owns and manages his own coffee house.

Gavin Reily is a New Orleans native. He is a graduate of the University of Mississippi and a country musician and songwriter now living in Nashville, Tennessee.

ACKNOWLEDGMENTS

The authors wish to thank the following:

Mike & Bree Drabicki for their work on the cover;

Brooke Lundy for loaning us her lips for the cover;

Mary Mazer of Art That Works;

Maryglenn McCombs of Dowling Press for her hard work;

and, last but not least, a special thanks to the women who served as inspiration for these rules.

I WROTE THE BOOK
ON DATING WOMEN!

MORE THAN
A Lifetime of Rules on
DATING WOMEN

*If you have any more rules on dating women,
please send them to:*
P.O. Box 121828 Nashville, TN 37212

*If we use your idea in our next book, we'll send
you this great T-shirt along with a free copy of*

MORE THAN *a Lifetime of Rules on* DATING WOMEN.

In case of duplicate submissions, the entry with the earliest postmark will be accepted.

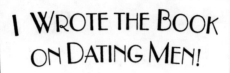

*If you have any rules on dating men,
please send them to:*
P.O. Box 121828 Nashville, TN 37212
*If we use your idea in our next book, we'll send
you this great T-shirt along with a free copy of*

A Lifetime of Rules on DATING MEN.

In case of duplicate submissions, the entry with the earliest postmark will be accepted.